Daily Prayers
in Islam

Basic Beliefs and How to Pray

The Light, Inc.
26 Worlds Fair Dr. Suite C
Somerset, New Jersey, 08873, USA
www.thelightpublishing.com

Title	Daily Prayers in Islam
Authors	Osman Bilgen - Ahmet Ozdemir
Editor	Jane Louise Kandur
Art director	Engin Ciftci
Published by	The Light, Inc.
Printed by	Caglayan A.S. - Izmir, 2006
ISBN	1-59784-005-X

Printed in Turkey

Publisher's Note: The accompanying Audio CD includes prayers and some short suras.

CONTENTS

Introduction

First of all in this guide, the proofs of the existence of Allah are presented in a simple and clear language. Then we go on to look at the steps leading to prayer, that is, purification and the call to prayer. Finally, we tried to briefly explain how to pray, in pictures and in words.

It may seem puzzling, at first glance; that this book does not deal with such issues as fasting, alms-giving, and pilgrimage. This prayer book has been prepared as a starter; therefore too much information has not been given at one time. The great Islamic scholar and thinker Said Nursi says "The highest truth after faith in God is prayer."

We hope that the readers who take the first step with the daily prayers become practicing Muslims in every way and they reflect the beauties of Islam in their life.

Belief in Allah, the prophethood, the day of Judgment, and the performance of the five daily prayers are the strong roots that keep us anchored in the ground, no matter how strong the wind blows.

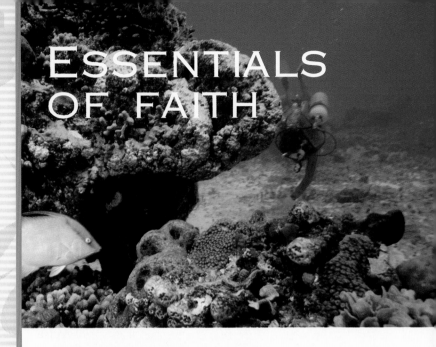

ESSENTIALS OF FAITH

1. BELIEF IN ALLAH

It is faith that makes man human, maybe even a sultan; It is thus man's major duty to believe and offer prayers…

Trees come into flower, ships travel on the sea, cows give us milk, the sun heats the earth… There is nothing useless on earth. Every part of creation, from the smallest atom, to the moon and the sun, has a mission; sometimes we can understand this mission, sometimes we cannot.

Human beings, the highest of Allah's creatures, think, speak, rejoice, worry… Why have human beings, the highest of creation, been created? What missions and purposes are human beings to accomplish? It is Allah, the Creator, Who knows human beings best. Therefore, we can discover the reasons for our creation from the Qur'an, which is the word of Allah. Allah says in the Qur'an: *"… I have not created the Jinn and humanity except to worship Me"* (Dhariyat 51:56).

How will we know Allah then? How will we learn about Him?

We can answer the question in this way: Allah lets us know about Himself in many various ways. The primary way is through the Holy Book, the Qur'an. Allah provides us with information about His attributes in the Qur'an. For example, we learn from Surat al-Ikhlas that He is One, and that all depend on Him while He depends on nothing, and also that nothing is like Him.

To read the Qur'an in order to become familiar with Allah's attributes is another form of worship.

Prophet Muhammad, peace and blessings be upon him, also told us about Allah and His attributes.

One of the ways to know Allah is to observe the universe. The universe is like a book that teaches us about our Lord, Allah. The earth we live on, all creation, whether alive or not, everything on the earth or in the sky has been created so perfectly that we automatically think that there must be a perfect being who has created all these things. This being is none other than Allah.

You might want to ask a question here: Isn't it possible for all these things to exist all by themselves? We don't see anyone make the flowers blossom, the sun rise, or the rain pour. So, why is it not possible for these things to all happen just by chance?

Well, think about it for a moment… When we see a letter written on a blank sheet, we know that someone must have written that letter. It is just possible that someone dropped their pen onto a piece of paper, and by chance a shape that looked like a letter was formed… What about the other letters on that paper? Were they also written by chance? How did these letters then line up to make a meaningful word? How did the letters come together to make a meaningful word, and the words to make sentences, and the sentences to make a book? Do we think that letters have a brain, that they know the topic of the book and line up in the correct way? Is this really possible? Let us turn to another example. Imagine a huge mosque, made up of many different stones. Did these stones know how to come together and make a beautiful building?

Of course we know that this is not possible. If there is a book, there has to be a writer... If there is a mosque, there must be a person who designed and built it. In the same way that a book can tell us who wrote it, and a mosque has an inscription telling us who built it, the universe tells us that someone has created it.

And this creator is Allah.

And if we think about it, we know that there can only be one Creator ... If you ask why, the answer is simple. We can see that all the things created cooperate with one another. Vitamin D is good for our bones. The fruit that trees give us tastes good. How does the sun know what our bones need? How does the apple tree know that we like apples? The same Creator has made the sun, the tree, and humans. If everything was created by someone different, there would not be such harmony among the creatures.

We said above that reading the Qur'an is also a type of worship. The universe is also a book of Allah - so, is it possible to say that reading the book of the universe is also a form of worship?

The answer to this question is "Yes!" It is a type of worship to think about the creation, to read and to see Allah's names and attributes in it. Many verses of the Qur'an tell us to reflect upon all the beauties of the universe and the way we have been created. And Prophet Muhammad, (pbuh), says that *"Reflection for an hour is more valuable than supererogatory prayers offered throughout the year"* (Al-'Ajluni, Kashf al-Khafa, 1:310).

The attributes of our Lord, Allah

The attributes of Allah are divided into two groups:

A- The Essential Attributes (al-Sifat al-Dhatiyyah):

1. al-Wujud: Allah is the Existing One.
2. al-Qidam: Allah is the Eternal in the Past. He existed before everything.
3. al-Baqah: Allah is the Eternal in the Future, He has no end.
4. al-Mukhalafatun-lil-Hawadith: Allah is not like the things He created.
5. al-Qiyam-bi-Nafsihi: Allah is the Self-Existing One. He is dependent on nothing else to exist.
6. al-Wahdaniyyah: Allah is the Unique One. He has no partner; He is not equal to anything.

B- The Immutable (Positive) Attributes (al-Sifat al-Thubutiyyah):

1. al-Hayat: Allah is alive. He is the Living One.
2. al-'Ilm: Allah knows everything. He is the All-Knowing One.
3. al-Iradah: Allah has unlimited power.
4. al-Qudrah: Allah is the Almighty and Omnipotent (All Powerful) One.
5. al-Sami': Allah hears everything. He is the All-Hearing One.
6. al-Baseer: Allah sees everything, be it hidden or not. He is the Omniscient (All-Seeing) One.
7. al-Qalam: Allah speaks in a unique way. He needs no sounds or letters.
8. al-Takwin: He is the Creator. He creates from nothing.

2. BELIEF IN THE ANGELS

The angels are also creatures of Allah. They are beings made from light, like spirits, but they can take on any form they wish to. As we learn in the Qur'an and from the hadiths (sayings) of the Prophet, angels do not need to eat or drink, they are neither male nor female, and they obey all of Allah's commands and prohibitions. It is only Allah Who knows how many angels there are. Four of these are "the Archangels." They are as follows:

1. Gabriel (Jibrail) (pbuh): It is his duty to give the orders of Allah to the prophets.
2. Michael (Mikail) (pbuh): He is responsible for managing the creatures and some natural phenomena.
3. Israfil (pbuh): He is responsible for starting apocalypse and resurrection of the dead.
4. 'Azra'il (pbuh): He is responsible for ending our lives. He is also called the Angel of Death.

There are also some angels with special duties. "Respected Recorders" (Kiraman Katibin) are busy recording all that we do, whereas Munkar and Nakir question the dead in the grave.

3. BELIEF IN THE BOOKS OR SCRIPTURES OF ALLAH

Allah, through Gabriel, at different times, gave to human beings holy books or smaller collections of pages (al-Suhuf) that let humans know what His commands and prohibitions are. The smaller collections of pages (al-Suhuf) were revealed to the following prophets:

- 10 pages were given to Adam (pbuh).
- 50 pages to Seth (pbuh).
- 30 pages to Enoch (Idris), (pbuh).

- 10 pages to Abraham (pbuh).

Here are the names of the Books and the prophets they were revealed:
- The Torah (Tawrat) to Moses (Musa), (pbuh).
- The Psalms (Zaboor) to David (Dawud), (pbuh).
- The Gospel (Injil) to Jesus (Isa), (pbuh).
- The Qur'an to Muhammad (pbuh).

The Qur'an is the final Book sent by Allah and Prophet Muhammad, (pbuh), is the final prophet. The Qur'an is the only one of Allah's Books that has been protected against change. It has kept to its original form and not a single letter of it will ever be changed.

4. BELIEF IN THE PROPHETS

The prophets are chosen people with special duties. They mediate between Allah and humanity. We are Allah's guests in this world for a short time. What does our Lord want us to do while we are His guests? Where will we go when our time as Allah's guests in this world ends? Allah sends the answers to these questions to human beings through His prophets.

The prophets are absolutely trustworthy and honest people. They relay the information and orders that they receive from Allah to humans.

The prophets are, like us, human beings. They eat, drink, rejoice, and worry… However, they have exceptionally good characters, and they have special attributes, given to them by Allah. These features are as follows:

1. **al-Ismah (Innocence, infallibility):** The prophets are virtuous people. Allah protects them from doing wrong. They do not commit sins.

2. **al-Amanah (Trustworthiness):** The prophets are trustworthy. They are reliable in all circumstances.

3. **Sidq (Truthfulness):** They never lie, even just for a joke. They are truthful in all circumstances.

4. **al-Fatanah (Intellect):** They have the highest degree of understanding, intelligence, and foresight.

5. **al-Tabligh (Communication):** They directly communicate divine messages to the people.

The prophets must have these qualities as the mission that they are given requires special characters. Islam is the final and the most perfect religion for humanity, which is why Prophet Muhammad, (pbuh), is the final prophet. He lived a life that is an example for all humanity, and completed his mission as a messenger of Allah.

We love Prophet Muhammad, (pbuh), very much. We follow his example, even in such everyday things as, drinking, sitting, and speaking; he has presented us with the perfect religion of Islam and taught us how to be good people. May Allah bless him and all the other prophets, as well as their companions. Amin.

5. BELIEF IN THE DAY OF JUDGMENT
(al-YAWM al-AKHIR)

We believe that we will rise from our graves to stand our final trial. This trial will be fair, but comprehensive. To do this is not a difficult task for our Creator, as He created us from nothing. Do we not see that many things burst into life all the time? The leaves drop in the winter, and trees appear to be dead. But come spring, and they turn green again. If even the trees can manage to come to life every spring, why shouldn't humans, Allah's perfect creatures, come to life again?

There are people who do wrong and cause others harm. We see that some people get away with bad or evil acts in this world. But we know that Allah will not let wrong acts go unpunished and that He will reward good deeds and punish bad ones in another place and time. This place, according to the Qur'an and the hadiths, is called the other world (akhirah). So, good Muslims do good actions and stop themselves from doing wrong, as we believe that good actions will be rewarded and bad ones punished on the Day of Judgment.

6. BELIEF IN THE DIVINE PREDESTINATION
(al-QADAR AND al-QADHA)

We have learnt that two divine attributes of Allah are "al-Qidam," which means that He is the Eternal in the Past, and "al-Baqah," which means He is the Eternal in the Future. This means that Allah is not a created being. He existed before everything and will exist after everything. He has no beginning or end.

Al-Qadar (Divine Destiny): This means that Allah's Knowledge includes all space and time. Everything exists in His Knowledge and He assigns to each a certain shape, life span, function or mission, and certain characteristics.

Al-Qadha (Divine Decree): This means that all events planned by Allah will occur at their due time.

We believe in al-Qadar and al-Qadha. This is why we put up with the difficulties that we are faced with in life, and we see these difficulties as being part of divine fate.

THE PILLARS OF ISLAM

Islam consists of five pillars:

1- Proclamation of faith (kalima al-Shahada): Being a Muslim begins with faith, and the basis of faith is to accept and believe. A person who wants to be a Muslim declares his/her belief by saying "Ash-hadu an la ilaha il-lal-lah, wa ash-ha du anna Muhammadan abduhu wa Rasuluhu" (I bear witness that there is no god but Allah, and I bear witness that Muhammad is His servant and Messenger).

2- Performing the prescribed prayers: Prayer (salat) is the first duty of a believer who has proclaimed faith. Prayer is widely dealt with in this work.

3- Prescribed alms (zakat): The word "zakat" literally means purification and increase. Giving the prescribed alms is a means for being purified from sins and for abundance in one's wealth. Any Muslim who is considered wealthy (possessing 85 grams of gold or more) after having assured their basic needs and sustenance should pay zakat. If a year has passed since the possession of the amount mentioned, the person who pays zakat should give (at least) one fortieth (%2.5) of his/her income to the needy.

4- Hajj (major pilgrimage): In the pilgrimage season, Muslims visit the Ka'ba and the sacred places around Makka and fulfill the duty of pilgrimage by completing the necessary forms of worship. Major pilgrimage should be performed by every Muslim who can afford it, once in their lifetime.

5- Fasting in Ramadan: Muslims fast during the month of Ramadan by abstaining from food, drink, and sexual intercourse starting from dawn to after sunset. Fasting develops feelings of compassion for others and encourages us to help those less fortunate than ourselves.

WUDU

Preparation for prayer (salat)

Muslims must make ablutions (wash certain parts of their bodies) in order to be able to pray, which is a fundamental part, or pillar, of Islam.

Muslims must wash certain parts of their body in running water before praying. This act is called wudu (ablution). By following the sunna we know how to make wudu.

There are four requirements of wudu. These are called the fard (obligatory) acts:

1. To wash the entire face, once.
2. To wash both arms thoroughly from wrist to elbow, once.
3. To wipe at least one fourth of the head with a wet hand.
4. To wash both feet up to the ankles.

For wudu to be counted these parts of our body must be washed at least once. The entire surface of relevant body parts are washed by moving garments or jewellery like rings. However, the most beautiful way is to make our wudu as Prophet Muhammad (pbuh) did. These acts are called the sunna acts of wudu.

1. We should start making wudu by reciting the audhu basmala. (Audhu billahi min ash shaitan erra jeem - Bismillahir Rahmanir Rahim). "Audhu" means "I seek refuge with Allah from the accursed Satan" and "Bismillahir Rahmanir Rahim" means "In the name of Allah, the Merciful, the Compassionate.")

2. To declare our intention to make wudu in order to pray.

3. To clean our teeth (by using a toothbrush, fingers, or a miswaq - a twig from a special type of tree that helps to clean our teeth).

4. To take water into our mouth and nostrils three times in a row.

5. To wash all the necessary parts of the body three times in a row.

6. To complete wudu without long intervals between washing each part of our body.

7. To wash the parts of our body in order.

8. To wipe our ears and the nape of our neck with wet fingers.

9. To pass a wet hand over our entire head.

10. To begin washing our feet from the tips of our toes.

Washing your hands :
Wash both of your hands up to your wrists. Make sure that the water goes between your fingers.

Washing your mouth:
Take water into your mouth three times, using your right hand. Rinse your mouth well each time before spitting out the water.

Sniffing water up into your nose:
Take water slightly up into your nostrils by sniffing, once again three times, using your right hand. Clear your nose using your left hand.

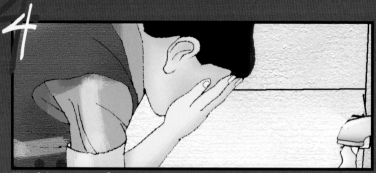

Washing your face :
Bring your two hands together and use a handful of water to wash your face three times from your forehead to the bottom of your chin, and then along the sides up to your ears.

Washing your arms :
Wash your right and left arms, each up to your elbow, three times.

Wiping your head :
Wet your right hand, and wipe at least one fourth of your head with it.

Wiping your ears :

Wet your hands and wipe the inside of your ears with the tips of the little finger, and wipe the back of your ears from bottom to top with your thumbs.

Wiping the nape of your neck :

Wipe the nape and the sides of your neck with the back of your wet hands.

Washing your feet :

Wash both feet, starting with the right one, including the ankles, with the help of your left hand. Make sure that the water goes between your toes.

Loss of wudu:

You will lose your wudu if any of the following happens:
1. If you go to the toilet or pass wind.
2. If you bleed, or if pus flows from a cut or sore.
3. If you vomit a mouthful or more.
4. If you lose consciousness.
5. If you fall asleep lying down.
6. If you become intoxicated.
7. If your gums bleed; the amount of blood must be as much as or more than the normal amount of saliva in your mouth.
8. If you laugh while praying so that someone else hears you.

Things that do not affect the wudu:

You do not lose your wudu if any of the following happens:
1. If your gums bleed, but the amount is less than the normal amount of saliva in your mouth.
2. If you cry.
3. If you cut or prick yourself lightly, and the blood does not flow.
4. If you shave, or cut your finger or toenails.
5. If you smile while praying.

Islam makes the performance of the religious practices easy. If you have a wound or a sore on any of the parts that must be washed during the wudu, whether or not it has a dressing, and if washing that part is likely to hurt you, you need only wipe over the injury or the dressing, rather than washing it. This should be done only once, not three times. If even wiping over the sore area will hurt you, then this does not have to be done either. The dressing does not have to be taken off to make wudu. This is true for both minor and major (complete) ablutions.

GHUSL

Ghusl means washing the entire body under running water. Sometimes this is an obligatory act (fard) and sometimes an advisable one, in accordance with the sunna of the Prophet. Sometimes you cannot perform your religious duties without having ghusl (complete ablution). Then ghusl becomes obligatory. Ghusl is sunna if, for example, you follow the Prophet's exercise of having a ritual bath every Friday before Friday prayer. Ghusl becomes obligatory for married couples after sexual intercourse, even if only the head of the penis disappears into the vagina. Any discharge of semen, even after a wet dream, and the completion of menses and post-childbirth bleeding.

The fard acts of ghusl:

1. Rinsing your mouth properly so that it is cleaned properly.
2. Taking water into your nose, right up to the bridge.
3. Washing your whole body.

How to make ghusl:

- You first have to recite the basmala (Bismillahir Rahmanir Rahim - In the name of Allah, the Merciful, the Compassionate) before making your intention, saying that you are cleaning yourself so that you can pray.

- Wash your hands, genital organs, and any other parts of the body that are unclean.

- Make wudu, as if you are going to pray (optional).

- Take a large amount of water into your mouth and into your nose, three times.

- Pour water three times over your head first, then over your shoulders, three times, starting with the right shoulder and scrubbing your shoulders each time.

- Finally your whole body should be washed in such manner that no dry spot remains.

Important things to remember when making ghusl:

- You must use running water.
- Difficult parts of the body, such as your earlobes, your navel, and underarms should be scrubbed to make sure the water has reached there.
- Your private parts should not be uncovered in front of others.
- You must be quiet and not say any prayer.
- You must not stand naked facing the Ka'ba, and your private parts must be covered.
- You should rub your scalp in order to make sure that the water reaches your hair roots.
- If water collects in a pool under your feet then you must wash your feet at the end.
- If you have a shower, instead of pouring water over your head three times, you need only to put your head and then your shoulders under the water and wash them for the same amount of time that it would take to pour water over your head three times.
- Ghusl is considered to cover wudu. If you make ghusl you can pray and perform other rituals that require wudu without needing to make wudu.
- If you do any of the things that cause you to lose wudu, it does not affect your ghusl, but you need to make wudu anew before doing anything that requires wudu, such as performing a prayer.

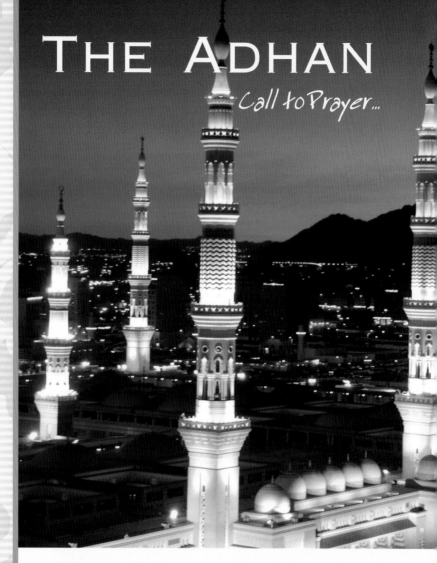

THE ADHAN
Call to Prayer...

The word for the call to prayer, adhan, which is called five times a day from the mosques, means literally to announce or declare. In our religion, it means the public recitation of certain words at certain times before obligatory prayers.

The adhan lets people know the start of the time period for a daily prayer or the time for a congregational service. Moreover, the words of the adhan glorify Allah and praise

Prophet Muhammad (pbuh) as the Messenger of Allah, also announcing that prayer is the door that leads to salvation. In order to call people for prayer, some companions of the Prophet (pbuh) proposed different methods such as using a bugle or ringing a bell. However, the Prophet (pbuh) did not accept these ideas, believing that the call to prayer would be more representative of the spirit of the prayer.

The adhan we hear today was first recited by one of the Prophet's companions, Bilal al-Habashi, with the approval of the Prophet. Here are the words of the adhan:

Allahu akbar	(Allah is the Greatest): 4 times
Ashhadu an la ilaha illa'llah	(I bear witness that there is no god but Allah): twice.
Ashhadu anna Muhammadan Rasulullah	(I bear witness that Muhammad is Allah's Messenger): twice
Hayya 'ala's-salah	(Come to prayer): twice.
Hayya 'ala'l-falah	(Come to salvation): twice.
Allahu akbar	(Allah is the Greatest): twice.
La ilaha illa'llah	(There is no god but Allah): once

Another call to prayer, said inside the mosque just before the actual start of the congregrational prayer is called *iqamah*. You also recite *iqamah* when you pray by yourself. The words of iqamah are the same as those of the adhan above, only with the addition of *"qad-qaamatis-salah"* (the prayer has begun), which is said twice after the second recitation of *"Hayya 'ala'l-falah."*

The adhan for fajr (early morning) prayer also has some extra words. The words *"assalatu khayrun minan nawm"* (prayer is better than sleep) are said twice after the second recitation of *"Hayya 'ala'l-falah."*

PRAYER

The pillar of our religion

Prayer is an act that both male and female Muslims must perform, five times every day. Prayer is such an important part of Islam that it is known as the center of worship. It is the most important way in which we can remember Allah. In the Qur'an it is written "... *so worship Me and keep up prayer for My remembrance*" (32:4, 6:80).

Prayer helps to organize a Muslim's daily life because we pray at five different times of day. Since we pray at certain times, prayer is a form of discipline, for both the body, the soul, and the character.

We pray because we have been ordered to do so by our Lord, Allah. All Muslim children who are seven years old should learn how to pray and they should begin praying regularly after they turn ten. We pray five times a day. The different prayers are the early morning (fajr) prayer, the noon (zuhr) prayer, the afternoon ('asr) prayer, the evening (maghrib) prayer and the late evening ('isha') prayer. Each of these prayers is to be performed during a certain time period. Each daily prayer is made up of different units (rak'at).

Three kinds of prayer: fard, wajib, and sunna:

Fard (obligatory) prayers: These are compulsory prayers. The fard prayers are the five daily prayers and the Friday prayer (offered in congregation); these prayers have to be performed, unless there is a legitimate reason for not praying.

Wajib (necessary) prayers: These include the two great festival ('iyd) prayers and the witr prayer. Many Muslim scholars consider wajib prayers as being no different from the fard prayers in terms of our being responsible for performing them.

Sunna prayers (those performed or advised by the Prophet): These include prayers that accompany the compulsory ones. They are called sunna prayers as they are the extra units of prayer offered originally by the Prophet (pbuh). Not performing these prayers is not a sin. However, the performance of sunna prayers makes Muslims feel closer to the Prophet (pbuh).

More about the five daily prayers:

Fajr prayer: This is offered in the time period from dawn until just before sunrise. It is made up of four units (rak'at), the first group of two being the sunna prayer and the last two being the obligatory (fard) prayer.

Zuhr prayer: This is offered in the time period from just after mid-day until mid-afternoon. It is made up of ten units; the first group of four being the sunna prayer, followed by a group of four units that is the fard prayer, and another group of two that makes up another sunna prayer.

'Asr prayer: This is offered in the time period from late afternoon until just before sunset. This consists of eight units, a group of four that makes up the sunna prayer followed by a group of four units that makes up the fard prayer.

Maghrib prayer: This is offered in the time period from after dusk until the full setting of the sun. It consists of five units. The first group of three is the fard prayer and the other group of two is the sunna prayer.

'Isha' prayer: This is offered in the time period that stretches from approximately one and half hours after sunset until midnight. It consists of 10 units; the first group of four being the sunna prayer, followed by a group of four that is the fard prayer, then by a group of two that makes up another sunna prayer.

Witr prayer: This is a wajib prayer offered after the 'isha' prayer. This consists of three units.

There are 12 requirements in order for a prayer to be counted; the first six requirements are called the Conditions of Prayer, and these should be observed before praying, while the other six are called the Obligatory Acts, or the Pillars of Prayer, which should be observed while praying.

Conditions of prayer:

1. Making ablution.
2. Ensuring that your body, clothing, and the area on which you are going to pray are all clean.
3. Dressing properly, so that the parts of the body that must be covered are covered (a man should cover his body from between, at least, the navel and the knees, while a woman should cover her entire body, except for her face, hands, and feet).
4. Offering the prayers at the correct times.
5. Performing the prayers in the direction of the qibla (Ka'ba).
6. Making an intention to perform a specific prayer.

The fard (obligatory) acts or the pillars of prayer:

1. You must start praying by reciting the (iftitah) takbir, Allahu akbar (Allah is the Greatest).
2. You must stand up (qiyam).
3. You must recite passages from the Qur'an (qiraah).
4. You must bow over, placing your hands on your knees (ruku').
5. You must prostrate (put your forehead on the ground while kneeling) (sajda).
6. You must sit upright in the final part (julus or tashah-hud).

The performance of prayer:

As we have already learnt about the times and units of the prayers, we may now look at how to perform the prayers.

Starting the Prayer

MALE

FEMALE

Face the qibla (the direction of the Sacred Mosque -Ka'ba- in Makka) in a clean place and make your intention to pray.

Start the Prayer with the Opening Takbir

MALE

Raise your hands up to your ears, with your palms open toward the qibla.

FEMALE

Raise your hands up to your shoulders. Placing your fingers together, open your palms facing the qibla.

Say Allahu akbar (Allah is the Greatest), and start to pray, placing one hand on top of the other.

Standing upright

MALE

Fix your eyes on the place where you will put your head rest during the sajda. Clasp your hands together, just below your navel, holding your left wrist by forming a ring with the thumb and little finger of your right hand.

FEMALE

Fix your eyes on the place where you will put your head rest during the sajda. Clasp your hands over your chest, the right hand on top of the left one.

MALE

FEMALE

While standing up recite "Subhanaka" and "al-Fatiha" (the opening sura of the Qur'an), followed by another portion from the Qur'an (for example, one of the last ten suras of the Qur'an). This recitation while standing up is called qiraah, which involves reciting a number of verses from the Qur'an.

Bowing

MALE	FEMALE

Make a full bow. Make sure your head and back are in a straight line. Put your hands on your knees with your fingers spread apart.

Slightly bow your head so that your back is slightly inclined, your head being higher than your hips. Your knees should be slightly bent. Put your hands on your knees with your fingers spread apart.

Say *"Subhana Rabbiya'l- 'Azim"* (Glory be to My Lord, the Greatest) three times.

Say *"Sami allahu liman hamida"* as you straighten up.

Say *"Rabbana walakal hamd"* when you stand upright.

Prostration

MALE

Place your head between your hands, making sure both your forehead and nose touch the ground. Position your elbows so that they are not in contact with the ground or the sides of your body. Make sure your heels are together.

FEMALE

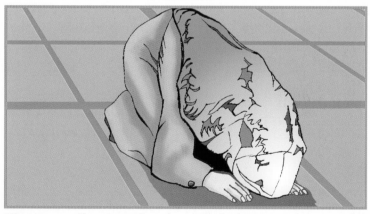

Place your elbows so that they touch the ground. Rest your stomach on your knees.

You do this action twice, one after the other. Say "Subhana Rabbiyal A'la" (Glory to My Lord, the Highest) three times when you put your forehead on the ground.

Sitting upright

MALE

FEMALE

Place the palms of your hands on your knees. Position your right foot so that it is straight, with toes bent in the direction of the Ka'ba.

Place the palms of your hands on your knees. Turn both feet out to the right. Place your left thigh on the ground.

Say the prayers *"at-Tahiyyatu," "Allahumma Salli-Barik,"* and *"Rabbana"* while in a sitting position.

Greeting

MALE

FEMALE

At the end of your prayer you turn your face to the right, with your eyes looking down at your right shoulder. Then turn your face to the left with your eyes looking down at your left shoulder.

Say "as-salamu 'alaykum wa-rahmatu'llah" (peace and the mercy of Allah be upon you) as you turn your head, both times. This act is called "a peace greeting."

THE CHART FOR DAILY PRAYERS

TYPE OF PRAYERS	UNITS (RAK'AT)	FAJR (Early Morning)	ZUHR (Noon)	ASR (Afternoon)	MAGHRIB (Evening)	'ISHA' (Late Evening)
		2 s. + 2 f.	4 s. + 4 f. + 2 s.	4 s. + 4 f.	3 f. + 2 s.	4 s. + 4 f. + 2 s. + 3
FIRST SUNNA	1	Subhanaka / Audhu-Basmala / Fatiha / Verse	Subhanaka / Audhu-Basmala / Fatiha / Verse	Subhanaka / Audhu-Basmala / Fatiha / Verse		Subhanaka / Audhu-Basmala / Fatiha / Verse
	2	Basmala / Fatiha / Verse / At-Tahiyyatu / Allahumma Salli wa Barik / Rabbana	Basmala / Fatiha / Verse / At-Tahiyyatu	Basmala / Fatiha / Verse / At-Tahiyyatu / Allahumma Salli wa Barik		Basmala / Fatiha / Verse / At-Tahiyyatu / Allahumma Salli wa Barik
	3		Basmala / Fatiha / Verse	Subhanaka / Auzu-Basmala / Fatiha / Verse		Subhanaka / Audhu-Basmala / Fatiha / Verse
	4		Basmala / Fatiha / Verse / At-Tahiyyatu / Allahumma Salli wa Barik / Rabbana	Basmala / Fatiha / Verse / At-Tahiyyatu / Allahumma Salli wa Barik / Rabbana		Basmala / Fatiha / Verse / At-Tahiyyatu / Allahumma Salli wa Barik / Rabbana
FARD	1	Subhanaka / Audhu-Basmala / Fatiha / Verse	Subhanaka / Audhu-Basmala / Fatiha / Verse	Subhanaka / Audhu-Basmala / Fatiha / Verse	Subhanaka / Audhu-Basmala / Fatiha / Verse	Subhanaka / Audhu-Basmala / Fatiha / Verse
	2	Basmala / Fatiha / Verse / At-Tahiyyatu / Allahumma Salli wa Barik / Rabbana	Basmala / Fatiha / Verse / At-Tahiyyatu	Basmala / Fatiha / Verse / At-Tahiyyatu	Basmala / Fatiha / Verse / At-Tahiyyatu	Basmala / Fatiha / Verse / At-Tahiyyatu
	3		Basmala / Fatiha	Basmala / Fatiha	Basmala / Fatiha / At-Tahiyyatu / Allahumma Salli wa Barik / Rabbana	Basmala / Fatiha
	4		Basmala / Fatiha / At-Tahiyyatu / Allahumma Salli wa Barik / Rabbana	Basmala / Fatiha / At-Tahiyyatu / Allahumma Salli wa Barik / Rabbana		Basmala / Fatiha / At-Tahiyyatu / Allahumma Salli wa Barik / Rabbana

TYPE OF PRAYERS	UNITS (RAK'AT)	FAYR (Early Morning)	ZUHR (Noon)	ASR (Afternoon)	MAGHRIB (Evening)	'ISHA' (Late Evening)
		2 s. + 2 f.	4 s. + 4 f. + 2 s.	4 s. + 4 f.	3 f. + 2 s.	4 s. + 4 f. + 2 s. + 3 w.
SECOND SUNNA	1		Subhanaka		Subhanaka	Subhanaka
			Audhu-Basmala		Audhu-Basmala	Audhu-Basmala
			Fatiha		Fatiha	Fatiha
			Verse		Verse	Verse
	2		Basmala		Basmala	Basmala
			Fatiha		Fatiha	Fatiha
			Verse		Verse	Verse
			At-Tahiyyatu		At-Tahiyyatu	At-Tahiyyatu
			Allahumma Salli wa Barik		Allahumma Salli wa Barik	Allahumma Salli wa Barik
			Rabbana		Rabbana	Rabbana
WITR	1					Subhanaka
						Audhu-Basmala
						Fatiha
						Verse
	2					Basmala
						Fatiha
						Verse
						At-Tahiyyatu
	3					Basmala
						Fatiha
						Verse
						Allahu Akbar
						Qunut Prayers
						At-Tahiyyatu
						Allahumma Salli wa Barik
						Rabbana

The following prayers are performed identically:

★ Sunna of Fajr - second sunna of Zuhr - sunna of Maghrib - second sunna of 'Isha'

★ Sunna of 'Asr - first sunna of 'Isha'

S: Sunna

F: Fard

W: Witr

FAJR (EARLY MORNING) PRAYER

Let us begin with the sunna prayer of the fajr prayer:

The two-unit sunna of the fajr prayer:

Make your intention, facing the qibla. Start your prayer with the opening takbir, saying "Allahu akbar." Recite Subhanaka, say the Audhu basmala. Then recite "al-Fatiha," and read a portion from the Qur'an.

Then bow down saying "Allahu akbar." While you are bowing, say "Subhana Rabbiya'l- 'Azim" three times. And then standing upright again, say these words: "Sami'allahu liman hamidah" (Allah accepts any who are thankful to Him). When you are standing upright again, say "Rabbana laka'l-hamd" (Our Lord, praise be to You).

Then prostrate, putting your forehead and nose to the floor, saying "Allahu akbar." This position is accompanied with the words "Subhana Rabbiyal A'la" three times. Then sit upright, saying "Allahu akbar." After a short rest in a sitting position make a second prostration, reciting the same phrases as you did in the first. Then stand up, saying "Allahu akbar," getting ready for the second unit of prayer.

In the second unit, clasp your hands again as you did in the first, and read "al-Fatiha," followed by a portion of the Qur'an before bowing.

While in the bowing position, say "Subhana Rabbiya'l- 'Azim" three times. Then stand up again, saying "Sami'a'llahu li-man hamidah." When fully upright, say "Rabbana wa-laka'l-hamd."

Then prostrate, putting your forehead to the floor again, saying "Allahu akbar," going on to say "Subhana Rabbiyal A'la" three times. Then, sit upright, saying "Allahu akbar." After a short rest in a sitting position make a second prostration, reciting the same phrases as before. Then rise to sit up, saying "Allahu akbar."

When in a sitting position offer the prayers of "at-Tahiyyatu," "Allahumma Salli-Barik," and "Rabbana." Then turn your face to the right and the left, in turn, looking down at your shoulder and saying "as-salamu 'alaykum wa-rahmatu'llah" each time. This is now the end of the sunna part of the fajr prayer.

The two-unit fard of fajr prayer:

The fard part of fajr prayer is also made up of two units, and is offered in the same way as the sunna part. However, boys and men should say the iqamah just before beginning the prayer. Let us now turn to other daily prayers.

ZUHR (NOON) PRAYER

The first four-unit sunna of zuhr prayer:

The first two units are performed in the same way as the sunna units of the early morning prayer. After reciting "at-Tahiyyatu" after the second unit, stand up and after saying the *basmala* recite "al-Fatiha" and a portion of the Qur'an. Then for the third and fourth units bow and prostrate as before. After finishing the fourth unit take up a sitting position to recite "at-Tahiyyatu," "Allahumma Salli-Barik," and "Rabbana." Then offer the peace greetings of "as-salamu 'alaykum wa-rahmatu'llah."

The four-unit fard of zuhr prayer:

The first two units are performed in the same way as the sunna units of the early morning prayer. After reciting "at-Tahiyyatu" after the second unit, stand up to recite the basmala, followed by "al-Fatiha." In both the third and fourth unit, no verses from the Qur'an need be recited after reciting the basmala and "al-Fatiha." Again, bow and prostrate in the same way as before. In the fourth unit, you only recite "al-Fatiha"; no other verses from the Qur'an are recited. Again, bow and prostrate in the same way as before, taking up a sitting position to recite "at-Tahiyyatu," "Allahumma Salli-Barik," and "Rabbana." Then offer the peace greeting of "as-salamu 'alaykum wa-rahmatu'llah" to end the prayer.

The second two-unit sunna of zuhr prayer:

This is done in the same way as the sunna units of the early morning prayer.

'ASR (MID-AFTERNOON) PRAYER

The four-unit sunna of the 'asr prayer:

The first two units are performed in the same way as in the sunna units of the early morning prayer. When sitting after the second unit, recite "at-Tahiyyatu," "Allahumma Salli-Barik," and "Rabbana" before rising to stand for the third unit. Start the third unit by reading "Subhanaka" before saying the audhu basmala. Continue to pray by reading "al-Fatiha" as you did for the four-unit sunna prayer of the noon prayer. After completing the four units; sit and recite "at-Tahiyyatu," "Allahumma Salli-Barik," and "Rabbana" before giving a peace greeting.

The four-unit fard of the 'asr prayer:

This is done in the same way as the four-unit fard of the noon prayer.

MAGHRIB (SUNSET) PRAYER

The three-unit fard of the maghrib prayer:

The first three units are performed in the same way as those of the fard of the zuhr prayer. But after the third unit you sit and recite "at-Tahiyyatu," "Allahumma Salli-Barik," and "Rabbana" before give the peace greeting in order to complete the prayer.

The two-unit sunna of the maghrib prayer:

This is done in the same way as in the sunna units of the early morning prayer.

'ISHA' (LATE EVENING) PRAYER

The four-unit sunna of the 'isha' prayer:

This is done in the same way as in the four units of the sunna of the late afternoon prayer.

The four-unit fard of the 'isha' prayer:

This is done in the same way as in the four units of the fard of the noon prayer.

The two-unit second sunna of the 'isha' prayer:

This is done in the same way as the sunna units of the early morning prayer.

WITR PRAYER

Witr is a wajib prayer and consists of three units. The first two units are performed in the same way as the sunna units of early morning prayer. After reciting "at-Tahiyyatu" in a sitting position after the second unit, rise for the third unit. In the third unit, say the basmala and read "al-Fatiha" followed by a portion from the Qur'an. Then raise your hands up to your ears as you do at the beginning of the prayer, saying "Allahu akbar" clasping your hands again to offer the prayer of "Qunut." Complete the prayer by bowing, prostrating, and sitting for the third unit, then reciting "at-Tahiyyatu," "Allahumma Salli-Barik," and "Rabbana," before offering the peace greeting.

JUM'A (FRIDAY) PRAYER

Apart form the five daily prayers there is also the jum'a prayer which is compulsory for male Muslims. This is a weekly gathering of the Friday congregation.

This prayer is performed in congregation. It is performed at the same time as (and instead of) the zuhr (noon) prayer. The jum'a prayer consists of ten units. The first four units are sunna, the middle two are fard, and the final two are sunna.

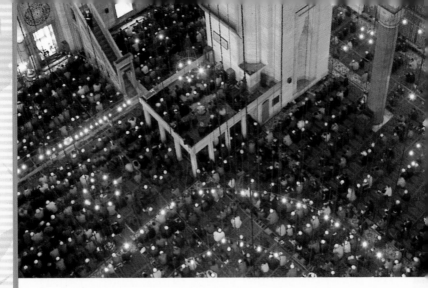

Performance of the jum'a prayer:

The four-unit first sunna of the jum'a prayer:

Make your intention to pray the first sunna of the jum'a prayer and perform these in the same way as the four-unit first sunna of the noon prayer.

The two-unit fard of the jum'a prayer:

The two-unit fard prayer is performed after the sermon (khutbah) has been read. After the sermon, the iqamah is called by the muezzin (caller to prayer) for the two-unit fard prayer. When the iqamah is almost finished the congregation rises to stand and makes their intention for the obligatory part of the jum'a prayer. The imam (leader of the prayer) says "Allahu akbar" out loud, while the congregation starts the prayer silently. The congregation recites "Subhanaka" while standing. "Al-Fatiha" and a portion of the Qur'an is recited by the imam out loud during both units. The congregation offers prayers in silence while bowing, prostrating, and sitting. The peace greeting of "as-salamu 'alaykum wa-rahmatu'llah" is recited along with the imam.

The four-unit final sunna of the jum'a prayer:

This is offered in the same way as the four-unit first sunna of the noon prayer.

Scholars also ruled that another prayer of four units, just like the four-unit fard of the noon prayer (with the intention of offering a later noon prayer) should be offered after the four-unit final sunna of the jum'a prayer. They also advise to follow this with another supererogatory prayer of two units with the intention of offering the sunna prayer for that time.

EID PRAYER

There are also eid prayers offered during the two religious festivals of eid al-Fitr (celebrated at the end of the month of Ramadan) and eid al-Adha (Festival of Sacrifice). These are considered wajib prayers for male members of the Muslim community. They are to be performed approximately forty-five minutes after sunrise.

Performance of the Eid prayer:

You make your intention and the opening takbir (Allahu akbar) with the imam. "Subhanaka" is recited silently. Then the imam raises his hands up to his ears and says "Allahu akbar." The congregation follows the imam, saying "Allahu akbar" in silence, before putting down their hands for a while. This act of raising your hands to your ears, saying "Allahu akbar" and then putting your hands down again is done three times. Bring your hands together after the third takbir. The imam then reads "al-Fatiha" and a portion of the Qur'an, leading the congregation to bow down and prostrate as in other prayers, before rising to stand for the second unit. In the second unit, the imam reads "al-Fatiha" and a portion of the Qur'an.

Then the imam and the congregation together repeat the act of takbir, raising their hands to their ears and saying "Allahu akbar," and putting their hands down again, three times. When the hands have been put down after the third takbir, the imam leads the congregation to bow down and prostrate as in the first unit, before rising to a sitting position to recite "at-Tahiyyatu," "Allahumma Salli-Barik," and "Rabbana." Then the peace greeting of "as-salamu 'alaykum wa-rahmatu'llah" is offered, following the imam. After the performance of the two units of the eid prayer the imam delivers a sermon.

The expression of the takbir of tashrik:

It is a wajib act to recite the takbir once after every fard prayer, starting from the early morning prayer on the eve of eid al-Adha (Festival of Sacrifice) until the mid-noon prayer on the fourth day. This takbir is called the "takbir of tashrik." It reads as follows: "Allahu akbar Allahu akbar, La ilaha ill'Allahu w'Allahu akbar, Allahu akbar walil-lahil-Hamd."

TARAWIH PRAYER

The tarawih prayer is performed after every 'isha' (late evening) prayer in the month of Ramadan only. It is considered to be a sunna prayer. The prayer consists of twenty units and can be performed individually or in congregation. It can be offered in units of two, or in units of four. If it is offered in units of two, then these are performed in the same way as the first two units of the sunna of the fajr prayer. If it is offered in units of four, then they are performed in the same way as in the sunna of the 'asr (afternoon) prayer.

CONGREGATIONAL PRAYER

It is recommended that fard prayers are offered in congregation, either at home or in the mosque. The rewards for praying in congregation are 27 times greater than those of prayers offered individually.

Performance of congregational prayer:

The imam stands about 1 meter in front of the congregation, facing the qibla. The imam reads "al-Fatiha" and a portion of the Qur'an out loud, while the congregation listens to him. However, the congregation offers all other prayers in silence. The congregation reads only "Subhanaka" in the first unit. It is a general rule that the congregation reads nothing in the other units while in the standing position, whether the imam reads out loud or silently, but offers other prayers while bowing, prostrating, and sitting in silence. Two people are enough to make a congregation. One leads the prayer and the other follows. If a congregation is formed by only two, a child or a girl can follow the imam. If someone joins the congregation in the middle of a prayer, he prays the parts he has missed after the imam has completed the prayer, after offering the peace greetings of "as-salamu 'alaykum wa-rahmatu'llah." If someone joins the congregation before or during the bowing he is considered to have prayed the unit to which the bowing belongs. The congregation is not supposed to say the takbir (Allahu akbar) or perform the acts of prayer before the imam says or does these things.

MORE TO KNOW ABOUT PRAYERS

Making up for qadha (missed) prayers:

Qadha means to make up for any prayer you may not have been able to pray at the proper time, because you have fallen asleep or maybe forgotten. All prayers should be prayed at their proper times, but if for some good reason you cannot, then you can make up for them later as qadha prayer.

Performance of qadha prayers:

The adhan and the iqamah should be called individually, and you should make your intention for the qadha of the prayer. Only the fard units should be prayed. Sunna prayers cannot be offered as qadha. If an early morning prayer cannot be offered at the proper time, it can be offered as qadha after sunrise the same day, along with the sunna as well.

Prayer during travel:

Islam makes things easier for those who are traveling. One of these is related to prayer. When someone is traveling with the intention of going further than 90 kilometers (around 60 miles) from home, then they can be considered "traveler" according to Islamic law. If they intend to stay there less than fifteen days, they shorten the four units of the fard prayers to two units during the journey or stay. They are not supposed to shorten the sunna units. They should perform these if they can. If not, they omit them. The fajr and the maghrib prayers, and also the witr prayer remain unchanged.

Sajdat-us sahw (prostration of forgetfulness):

This is extra prostration offered to make up for omitting or forgetting a part or parts of the prayer. If you postpone one of the fard (obligatory) acts, or omit one of the wajib acts, then you must offer two prostrations upon completion of the prayer. This is done at the end of the last unit of the prayer. After reciting "at-Tahiyyatu" you turn to the right for the peace greeting of "Assalamu 'alaykum," and then perform two extra prostrations, each beginning with "Allahu akbar." After these prostrations you sit upright to offer "at-Tahiyyatu," "Allahumma Salli-Barik," and "Rabbana" before completing your prayer with the peace greetings.

Sajdat-ut Tilawat (prostration upon reading):

There are 14 verses of the Qur'an that when one hears or reads them they must offer sajdatu tilawat, whether you are praying at the time or not.

Performance of sajdat-ut tilawat:

Make your intention and prostrate, without raising your hands, and say "Subhana Rabbiyal A'la" (Glory to My Lord, the Highest) three times, then stand up. After standing up, it is advisable to say "Ghufranaka rabbana wa ilayka'l-Maseer," meaning "Your forgiveness (do we crave), and to You is the eventual return."

The makruh (undesirable) acts in prayer:

A makruh act is an undesirable act, but it is not a sin. Regarding prayer, the following acts are seen as makruh:

1. Praying when you need to go to the toilet.
2. Playing with your clothes or parts of your body.
3. Leaning against something (a wall, a tree, etc.).
4. Stretching or yawning.
5. Cracking your knuckles.

These acts do not nullify one's prayer, but reduce its rewards. There are also acts that invalidate prayer.

Acts that invalidate prayer:

1. Speaking or laughing in prayer.
2. Turning your chest away from the direction of the Ka'ba.
3. Acting in such a way that someone watching would not know that you were praying.
4. Uncovering your private parts.
5. Eating or drinking.

The wajib (necessary) acts of prayer:

1. Starting a prayer with the recitation of "Allahu akbar."
2. Reciting "al-Fatiha."
3. Reciting "al-Fatiha" before a portion of the Qur'an.
4. Touching your forehead and nose to the ground while prostrating.
5. Reciting "at-Tahiyyatu" at all sittings.
6. Completing the prayer with the peace greetings.
7. Observing the advisable manners of prayer.

The sunna acts of prayer:

1. Calling the adhan and the iqamah for the five daily and Friday prayers.
2. Raising the hands up while saying "Allahu akbar" to start your prayer.
3. Reciting "Subhanaka" and the audhu basmala in silence.
4. Saying "Amin!" at the end of "al-Fatiha."
5. Keeping the knees straight when bowing (for males).
6. Reciting "at-Tahiyyatu" in silence.
7. Placing a sutrah (barrier) in front of you when praying in an open area.

NOTES